SHEFFIELD
IN THE SEVENTIES

SHEFFIELD
IN THE SEVENTIES

PETER GOODMAN

breedon books
PUBLISHING

First published in Great Britain in 2002 by
The Breedon Books Publishing Company Limited
Breedon House, 3 The Parker Centre,
Derby, DE21 4SZ.

ISBN 1 85983 335 7

Printed and bound by Butler & Tanner, Frome, Somerset, England.

Cover printing by Lawrence-Allen Colour Printers, Weston-super-Mare,
Somerset, England.

Contents

Acknowledgments

My grateful thanks are due to many people, not least the Sheffield Newspapers photographers who worked for *The Star* and *Morning Telegraph* in the 70s.

Their professional expertise is reflected in the high standard of the photographs in the book and particularly noticeable is the 'newsy' aspect of many of the pictures.

As with reporters, newspaper photographers need to have a nose for the news angle in a picture because it is this quality which lifts the image above the ordinary and gives it reader appeal.

So my thanks to them for allowing me the opportunity to project their work in this book about the 70s.

I am grateful, too, to the readers of *The Star* who have shared their 70s memories with us and contributed photographs. I feel that this particular chapter of the book belongs to them and is, therefore, very special.

I also appreciate very much the valuable assistance I have received from Sheffield Newspapers staff, particularly Christine Chan, Helen Faley, Nicola Ball and Angela Furniss. Without them, the compilation of this book would have been much more difficult.

Introduction

Welcome to Sheffield in the Seventies!

It seems only a short step back in time – until you realise that any Sheffielder under 35 probably won't remember Fargate when traffic ran through it, the landmark Grand Hotel on Leopold Street where visiting celebrities stayed, Davy's famous restaurant and popular meeting place on Fargate, the Vogue Cinema at Sheffield Lane Top, the jingle of sixpences and threepenny bits in your pocket as you set off for a night out...

Neither will they recall the days before the Parkway linked the city to the M1 or the industrial problems and power shortages which led to television having to finish at 10.30pm and motorists not being able to drive over 50mph.

Not to mention Billy Smart's circus, Yorkshire playing cricket at Bramall Lane football ground and the sheer artistry of Tony Currie and Willie Henderson as they thrilled crowds at Sheffield United and Wednesday respectively.

The early Seventies were the days when T-shirts came without slogans and it was legal to drive without seatbelts. Streakers ripping their clothes off at sports events hadn't been heard of.

And it wasn't until 1970 that you were allowed to vote at 18 instead of 21.

The decade wasn't without its freak weather either. In 1975, snow actually stopped play at a cricket match – in June! Then followed two of the hottest summers in memory.

What nobody noticed halfway through the decade was a 19-year-old computer whiz called William Henry Gates dropping out of college in America in 1975 to start his own business. He was a bit quicker than the rest of us and finished up a billionaire before he was 30.

Even this briefest of reviews of the things we lost and gained in the Seventies serves as a reminder that time has rushed on, played tricks with our memories and persuaded us that from then to now was a mere cockstride.

So enjoy looking back to Sheffield in the Seventies and the many photographs which reflect that era. There are hundreds of identifiable faces in the book – and yours might just be one of them!

Peter Goodman
September 2002

City Snapshots

Shopping Bliss In Traffic-Free Fargate!

SHOPPERS enjoyed the sheer pleasure of being able to stroll along Fargate without the worry of traffic when it became a pedestrian precinct in February 1971.

It happened at a time when Sheffield was projecting itself to the outside world as a developing city and in March 1971 a week-long City On The Move exhibition opened at the Royal Exchange in London.

And there was something else new for Sheffielders to get used to two weeks after Fargate had become pedestrianised – decimalisation.

In that same month, the Grand Hotel in Leopold Street closed, overtaken by new hotels such as the Hallam Tower which had opened in 1965.

A year later, another familiar landmark and popular meeting place, Davy's shop and restaurant on Fargate, closed for business.

Work started on the "egg box" Town Hall extensions in 1972 and their appearance met with a mixed response from city folk.

"Absolutely dreadful", said some. "Wonderful", was the verdict of others.

They lasted 30 years and were demolished in 2002.

As the decade ended, The Moor went the way of Fargate as traffic was diverted round it and pedestrian power won the day.

The 'road closed' sign marks the end of through traffic on Fargate in 1971.

Sunshine, trees, pleasant walking areas…
Fargate in 1974. Note the subway, now no
more, which linked Fargate with the other
side of High Street.

Tidying up in June 1974. By this time, Fargate
was firmly established as a pedestrian
precinct.

Christmas 1977 as
shoppers on Fargate search
for last-minute bargains.

Another Christmas shopping
scene on Fargate, this time
1974.

20 January 1978, and shoppers throng Fargate.

A busy scene on Exchange Street in January 1978.

Sunbathers relax in the Peace Gardens in the summer of 1975.

The Moor in 1979 and seats for the weary have taken the place of traffic. It's a peaceful scene and the two cyclists do nothing to disturb it.

The Star billboard says it all. This picture, from April 1977, shows workmen cleaning up the Goodwin Fountain following an article in *The Star* about its unkempt state. The picture below was taken two weeks later. What a transformation!

The Moor in 1976, three years before it was pedestrianised.

New city centre traffic regulations, including the closure of High Street to any vehicles other than buses and those delivering to shops, were introduced in 1973. This picture shows police at the end of High Street diverting traffic coming off the Arundel Gate island.

A quiet High Street in 1973 after through traffic, apart from buses and delivery vehicles, had been banned.

Fitzalan Square in April 1978.

A panda car surveys the scene in Fitzalan Square during an April evening in 1976. Note the Classic Cinema, no longer there, in the centre of the photograph.

A scene on Haymarket in May 1972.

The city centre at night? No, just a very dismal morning in December 1971.

This was once the main entrance to the *Telegraph* and *Star* building at the junction of York Street and High Street before the offices were moved further down York Street. The building is now occupied by the Bradford and Bingley Building Society and this photograph of the frontage being demolished was taken in 1971.

Angel Street in 1971 with the Hole in the Road prominent to the top left of the picture.

The City Hall takes centre stage in this picture of Barker's Pool in 1976.

The Wicker at the start of the decade. The photograph was taken from the Wicker Arches.

David Blunkett, now Home Secretary, was one of the councillors who helped shape developing Sheffield in the 70s. He is pictured with his guide dog in 1978.

The once-grand Grand Hotel bowed out in 1971. This exterior shot was taken a year earlier, in 1970.

Wilson, Heath, Thatcher visit Sheffield

All three 70s Prime Ministers, Harold Wilson (1964-70 and 1974-76), Ted Heath (1970-74) and Maggie Thatcher (1979-90), visited Sheffield during the decade but not necessarily while they were holding office.

There was snow on the ground and plenty of winter woollies on show when Prime Minister Harold Wilson paused to chat to children from Parkhill Junior and Infants School outside the Grace Owen Nursery School, Parkhill, in January 1970.

Maggie Thatcher was here in July 1972 to open the Dronfield Henry Fanshawe School extensions and again in March 1975 to visit local factories.

Ted Heath came to Sheffield in November 1976, to autograph copies of his two books, on Sailing and Music. He is pictured here at Taylors Bookshop, Broomhill, Sheffield.

During his November 1976 visit to Sheffield, Ted Heath also presented prizes at Sheffield's High Storrs School speech day.

Children of the 70s

Happy, Smiling Faces – And That's A Promise!

THERE'S nothing more appealing, particularly to mums and dads, than photographs of children and this section of the book is devoted to youngsters from the 70s doing what they do best – enjoying themselves.

Many of the pictures were taken at the annual Sheffield Whit Sings when children and adults from local churches walked in procession to the parks to celebrate their faith and have a 'real good sing'.

They were joyous occasions and the highlight of the year for thousands of families. Sheffield Newspapers photographers looked forward to them, too, because they knew they were guaranteed pictures of happy, smiling faces.

Many of the churches elected Sunday School queens and attendants to head the processions and some are featured in the following selection of photographs.

Hollinsend, Sheffield, Whit Sing in 1975 and these little songstresses are singing from the same hymn sheet.

Traditionally, the Weston Park Whit Sing always attracted one of the biggest crowds of the day and 1975 was no exception.

Children and adults from Wesley Hall Church, Crookes, Sheffield, at the 1974 Whit Sing in Weston Park.

Endcliffe Park, Sheffield, in 1974 and judging by the lovely wide smile on her face this little girl has just been crowned queen.

Up pops a photographer from *The Star* at the 1971 Weston Park Whit Sing and these young ladies are overcome with a fit of the giggles!

This lovely study was taken at the 1974 Sheffield Firth Park event.

Star photographer Stuart Hastings was responsible for this superb picture at Meersbrook Park in 1972.

Thirteen-year-old Gillian Robinson, of Walkley, was crowned queen of the Sheffield Christian Education Council West Branch at the 1970 Weston Park Whit Sing. She is pictured here with her attendants – her sister Deborah, aged 10, and nine-year-old Sandra Smalley.

Joining in the singing at the 1970 Meersbrook Park event are Susan Tomlinson, queen of Ebenezer Wesleyan Reform Church, Bramall Lane, and her attendants Evelyn and Sharon Thomas.

Sisters Yvette and Michelle Smith, aged six and five, acted as attendants for 15-year-old Elsa Forsythe, queen of Victoria Hall Methodist Church, at the 1971 Norfolk Park Whit Sing.

Picture shows (from the left) Alison Stead, aged eight, Wendy Burnage, 10 and Joanne Frost, eight, at Hillsborough Park in 1978. The three Girl Guides were all members of the 23rd (Wisewood) company.

Children and adults from churches in the Intake district of Sheffield assembled at Hollinsend Recreation Ground for the 1977 Whit Sing.

The little girl on the front row to the right of the picture is singing with great gusto at the 1978 Firth Park Whit get-together.

The venue isn't known but this picture was taken at a Sheffield Whit Sing in 1978.

It's 1971 and the Easter school holiday is nearly over. So the editor's brief to photographer Stuart Hastings was to come back to the office with a picture reflecting back-to-school gloom. It looks like he succeeded…

Fun times at a playground in Broomhall, Sheffield, in 1974.

Saying their prayers in 1976 are (left) Lisa Stokes, aged five, and Wendy Crossley, also five, both of Totley, Sheffield.

Spellbound children watch an open air performance of 'St George and the Dragon' in 1979.

It's bath time for the dolls at Broomhall Nursery School, Sheffield, in 1978.

Just look at that mess! Toddlers from Dronfield Woodhouse Play Group helped to paint a background in Walsh's shop window in Sheffield in 1974 to promote a painting competition organised by a children's clothes company. Love the wellies!

Having fun in the playing field next to Brampton Bierlow Parish Hall in 1973 are, from left, Maxine Rawson, aged 10, Christine Veasey, nine, and Tracey Birley, eight.

Admiring the nativity crib at Sheffield Midland Station in December 1971, are Mrs Patricia Kennedy, from Whiston, Rotherham, and her two-year-old daughter Carey.

Walking tall are these children on a play scheme in Sheffield's Stannington Park in August 1975.

You can fair hear the noise these youngsters are making at Parson Cross Park, Sheffield, in August 1975.

Fun times at the Crookes Valley Park playground, Sheffield, in June 1976. Looks like they're trying to set a record for the most children on a roundabout!

'There's no more when this has gone' – three-year-old Jennie Dibb, of Hunters Bar, Sheffield, feeds the ducks at Endcliffe Park, Sheffield, in December 1974.

Toys galore for children from Sheffield Central Congregational Church Play Group in 1973.

Two-year-old Karl Wayne Morris, from The Star Inn, Rawmarsh, cuddles his pet St Bernard which is as tall as he is! The picture was taken by photographer Geoff Tyrer in 1973.

A lollipop lady shepherds children across the road in Sheffield in June 1978.

Somewhere in Sheffield in August 1974. The venue is unknown but what isn't in doubt is the sheer joy on the faces of these youngsters.

The Shipley quads from Sheffield were big news in 1970. Mum Maureen and dad Derek look on proudly as (from left) Richard, Paul, Elizabeth and Adrian line up for a photocall.

Gloops Makes A Comeback For Junior Star

During the 70s, *The Star* had a thriving Junior Star section which involved Sheffield children in a wide variety of activities including football coaching, charity collections, packing parcels for old people at Christmas, preserving wildlife, days out and concerts.

Gloops, the famous cartoon cat featured in *The Star* mainly in the 40s and 50s, made a re-appearance in the 70s, not in *The Star* as such but 'in person' at many Junior Star events. Older readers of *The Star* still talk fondly of the Gloops Club and many still have their membership cards.

The following photographs cover a selection of Junior Star activities from the 70s.

Gloops launches the balloon race at Sheffield Norfolk Park School garden fete in July 1974. Watching the balloon drifting into the sky is fete organiser Irene Huff, chairman of the Norfolk Park School Hydrotherapy Pool Fund.

Gloops steals the show from Father Christmas at St Augustine's Christmas Fair, Sheffield, in 1974.

Gloops the gardener! Children planted 50 trees on East Bank Road, Sheffield, in March 1973, and Gloops was there to help Colin Brannigan, then editor of *The Star*, unveil a commemorative plaque.

Christmas 1972 and Gloops is thrilled to receive a Christmas present from Father Christmas at Woodseats Police party, Sheffield.

Gloops goes Raving Bonkers at Redgates toy store in Sheffield in 1973, playing the fighting robots game with seven-year-old Karen Toseland, of Vincent Road, Sheffield.

Gloops helped to switch on Sheffield's Christmas Illuminations in 1972 and was rewarded with a kiss from television personality Hughie Green.

Fame at last! Gloops meets Harry Corbett with Sooty and Sweep in Sheffield in 1974.

Four members of Junior Star put their best feet forward in October 1975, and raised £12 for the PDSA from a sponsored walk. They are (from left): April Slingsby aged seven (with Digby the hamster), Alison Slingsby 10, Julia Sturdy 12, and Susan Sturdy 11, all of Hollythorpe Road, Sheffield.

Junior Star organised regular football coaching for youngsters and in October 1975, Councillor George Wilson, leader of Sheffield City Council, presented certificates to 450 of them at the gymnasium at Hillsborough Football Ground.

Quite a comic was Junior Star member Deborah Gledhill, aged nine, of Woodland View, Gleadless, Sheffield, in 1975 – she had 1,200 of them in her collection.

Reporters in the making? For a couple of days in May 1973, the sons and daughters of *The Star's* journalists took over the desks normally occupied by their mums and dads to write and produce the Junior Star section. Some readers said they noticed an improvement!

The Saturday night *Green 'Un* sports paper has long been regarded as one of the country's best for the quality of its content and the speed of its output. Its delivery boys and girls form an important part of the team and this picture was taken in August 1975 just before the start of the new football season.

Making news themselves in 1970 were these finalists in the Telegraph and Star's Newsboy and Girl competition. Holding the trophy in the middle of the photograph is overall winner Anthony Mannion.

The Star's promotional caravan with its Paper Dollies was a familiar sight in the 70s at events throughout the Sheffield and South Yorkshire area and making friends with local children in this picture are Judi Walker (left) and Dawn Kendall.

Your Memories
– Star Readers Recall The 70s

The Bride And Bridesmaids Were In Stitches – Thousands Of Them!

It was a beautiful wedding and the bride and bridesmaids, who were in stitches throughout the ceremony and the reception, looked absolutely gorgeous.

For Lesley Waller used 200 balls of wool to crochet five dresses, including her own, for her wedding at Heeley Parish Church, Sheffield, on 10 March 1973. The bride's dress even appeared on television later in a Consumer Protection programme!

Lesley and her bridesmaids outside Heeley Parish Church, Sheffield, in March 1973. From the left are: Lesley's sister Tina Hill, June Waller, Carol Lee and, holding Lesley's train, Sharon Collis.

Lesley, of Hackthorn Road, Woodseats, recalls: 'Crochet work had become popular in the early 70s, not for the traditional lacy edgings and mats as in the past, but for clothes. I crotcheted many dresses for myself and others so when I saw a pattern in a magazine for a crocheted wedding dress, I just had to have it.

'The task began in May 1972 with 85 balls of wool which cost £7.65. The outfit consisted of a long straight sleeveless dress with a jacket tapering from the front into a train at the back. It was with the last two back sections of the train where I hit a problem.

'The pattern and its complex tapering did not work out. This must have been December/January time and I didn't know what to do. The magazine who printed the pattern were not helpful so, in despair, I wrote to the Weights and Measures Department at Sheffield Town Hall.

'They took the matter up with the company, Robin Wools, whose wool was suggested for the pattern and they agreed to sort the matter out. I posted the entire jacket and train to them and they said they would complete it for me.

Lesley, in stitches and in love, with husband Neil.

'They did but it was a close thing. It didn't arrive at Sheffield Station until the Wednesday before the wedding on the Saturday.'

And while Robin Wools were completing the dress, Lesley was pressing on with the four bridesmaids' dresses, using a total of 200 balls of wool.

Some months later, Valerie Singleton was preparing a television programme on consumer protection and asked if she could use Lesley's wedding dress as an example of the type of problem they took up on behalf of the public.

Wedding Bliss in Early 70s

Happy times in the early 70s are recalled by Margaret Otter, of Hollybank Way, Sheffield. She married husband Tony in May 1971. Tony worked as a fitter for the East Midlands Gas Board for 30 years.

Margaret and Tony's wedding in May 1971.

Margaret in her hotpants suit in July 1971.

Margaret and Tony pictured at the wedding of Tony's friend, Ron Brookes, in October 1970.

Paddling To Happiness

Happy times at Millhouses Park, Sheffield, paddling pool are recalled by Sheila Tidy, of Manor, Sheffield. She says: 'Those were the days! A trip to Millhouses Park was a great day out.'

In the forefront of the photograph is Sheila's daughter Philippa and her friend Adrian. The picture was taken in 1977.

Julie's First Pair Of Hotpants

Hotpants were all the fashion rage in the early 70s and Julie Beardshaw, of Trenton Close, Woodhouse, Sheffield, looked stunning when she wore her first pair in June 1971. Julie was 21 at the time and on honeymoon in Skegness.

Julie on honeymoon in her yellow hotpants outfit in 1971.

A Special Day In 1973

28 July 1973 was a very special day for Mrs C. Briggs and husband Graham, of Jenkin Avenue, Wincobank, Sheffield. They were married at St Barnabas Church, Highfields, Sheffield. Best man was Philip Weaver and the bridesmaids were Sandra Baxter and Paula and Joanne Daly. Mrs Briggs' cousin Brian Daly gave her away.

The wedding party in 1973.

A Dedicated Follower Of Fashion

Keeping up with fashion was all part of the excitement in the 70s and Trisha Broadhead, of Providence Road, Sheffield, says: 'We considered ourselves to be very fashionable – I certainly did with flared trousers, tank top, clogs and a "page boy" haircut!'

Trisha and husband Len, then her fiance, pictured by the duck pond in Endcliffe Park in September 1972.

Comic Opera Society Raises Funds For New Crucible Theatre

Sheffield's City Comic Opera Society staged *Yeomen of the Guard* at the Montgomery Theatre in 1971 in aid of the city's new theatre, the Crucible, which opened in November 1971. The show ran for a week and was sold out every night. It resulted in a cheque for £262 being handed over to the Crucible.

These two photographs were sub-

The cast of "Yeomen of the Guard" pictured at Sheffield's Montgomery Theatre in 1971.

Sheffield City Comic Opera Society musical director Gertrude Stockil presents a cheque for £262 to David Brayshaw from the Crucible Theatre management.

mitted by Margaret Stringfellow, then Margaret Watkinson, of Lees Hall Road, Sheffield, who was the Society's patronage secretary for 50 years and responsible for ticket sales.

The Society folded in 1993 but friendships from those days live on. Once a fortnight, Margaret gets together with Barbara Jenks, who was Society chair, Joan Howarth (wardrobe mistress), Joan Robinson, principal contralto, and Jean Blackburn who worked with Margaret in the box office.

Says Margaret: 'They were happy days and the memories were very special.'

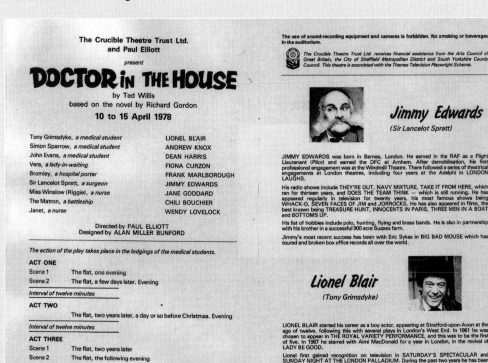

A 1978 programme from the Crucible Theatre – Jimmy Edwards and Lionel Blair starring in Doctor In The House. The programme is reproduced from Margaret Stringfellow's collection.

The Sheffield Polytechnic Eric Mensforth Library starts to take shape in 1973.

New Polytechnic Library Takes Shape

This fine picture from 1973 shows the Sheffield Polytechnic (now Hallam University) Eric Mensforth Library in the early stages of construction.

The library, on Pond Street, was designed in the office of the Department of Planning and Design, City of Sheffield Metropolitan District Council, by Don Glenn who was the project architect.

Don, of Stannington, Sheffield, kindly supplied this photograph. The building was officially opened in 1975.

Pond Street bus station is on the left of the picture, as is Sheaf Valley Baths opened in 1972 by entertainer Rolf Harris.

The entrance to the Midland Station is just off the picture top right.

Special Brownie Event Sets Diane Thinking

As a youngster growing up in the 70s, Diane Glenn has a host of memories that will stay with her for the rest of her life, including her time in the Brownies.

Diane, from Stannington, Sheffield, whose father was project architect for the Sheffield Polytechnic Eric Mensforth library which opened in 1975 (see previous item) particularly remembers a "Thinking Day" ceremony at Sheffield City Hall on February 11, 1973, and has sent us this picture.

Diane, who was a member of the 163rd Brownie pack from Stannington, is third from the left on the front row holding a flag and wonders what became of the other happy faces on the photograph..

Self-help Project Kept Children Dry

A 70s do-it-yourself school project to keep children dry as they switched from one classroom to another is recalled by Doreen Stephenson, of Charnock, Sheffield.

A group of parents whose children were pupils at Charnock Hall School got together to build a brick and glass corridor, using the skills of dads who had joiners, a bricklayer, a plumber and a surveyor in their ranks.

They swung into action when the Education Department said it couldn't allocate any money to the project.

This picture came from Doreen's friends Trevor and Hilary Bruce who were also involved in the project.

Doreen, whose husband Graeme sadly died in 1989, still has a grand daughter, Emma, at the school. Doreen's daughter and son both went to Charnock Hall School as did Trevor and Hilary's two boys.

The do-it-yourself project starts to take shape. Pictured are Trevor Bruce, Bill Clark, Graeme Stephenson, Dennis Walters and Eric Copley.

Television 'stardom' for sisters Rebecca and Ruth

Rebecca (left) and Ruth Commander at Bournemouth in 1975. Ruth is holding her silver cup, which she still has, for winning a Beautiful Baby competition. Another of her prizes was a bottle of bubbly to match her personality!

Little Ruth Commander's curly hair, bonny face and bubbly personality swept the judges off their feet when she entered a Beautiful Baby competition in Bournemouth in August 1975.

Just 18 months old and on holiday with mum Carol, dad Tony and big sister Rebecca, aged four, she won the 0-2 years category in the contest held during the Boscombe and Bournemouth Regatta Week.

Four years later, Rebecca and Ruth were taken on their first cruise, sailing on the Oriana in the Mediterranean, and a chance meeting on deck with Jimmy Savile led to them appearing on the *Jim'll Fix It* television programme no fewer than seven times!

Mum Carol, of Stannington, explained: 'We became quite friendly with him during the cruise and on returning home he rang us and invited the girls to appear on his August Bank Holiday special.

'The following month he was doing a national charity run, taking in 30 different cities including Sheffield and he invited us all to the Grosvenor House Hotel for tea.'

During the *Jim'll Fix It* shows, Rebecca and Ruth met many celebrities including Status Quo and snooker supremo Steve Davis.

Rebecca and Ruth take tea with Jimmy Savile at Sheffield's Grosvenor House Hotel in 1979.

More Than 50 In Wedding Group

22 July 1972, holds special memories for Ted Maidment. It was the day he married Patricia Langstaff at St Peter's Church, Base Green, Sheffield. Says Ted, of Harwood Gardens, Waterthorpe Estate, Sheffield: 'As you can see from the photograph, quite a few of the guests are making 70s fashion statements.'

There are more than 50 people on this happy wedding photograph from 22 July 1972, when Ted Maidment married Patricia Langstaff.

Weather in the 70s

It Was So Cold We Gritted Our Teeth...
But They Hadn't Gritted The Roads!

ALTHOUGH the Sheffield area didn't experience any repeat of the terrible weather extremes of the 60s, such as the hurricane winds of 1962 which killed four people and injured many others, or the intense bitterness of the 1962-63 winter which went down on record as the worst of the 20th century, the 70s did have its moments.

During the long, hot summer of 1976, for instance, we seemed to eat, and sometimes sleep, outside every night. Barbecues could be planned well in advance with little or no thought of a late cancellation because of a downpour and offices gave serious consideration to creating outside working areas for their baking, boiling staff.

Perma-brown bodies – skin cancer warnings were hardly heard of then – and parched lawns testified to the heat and pupils at King Edward VII School, Sheffield, threw their caps in the air when they were sent home early for several days because of soaring classroom temperatures.

Being likened to tender young chickens rotating on a spit was not their idea of fun. Neither was homework and more than one inventive pupil must have used the excuse that his or her ball point pen had dried up in the heat.

The temperature reached 86 degrees on June 29, the area's hottest day since the 1950s, and everybody and everything overheated including cars and buses.

At the other end of the thermometer, we gritted our teeth to face the bitter cold of the 1978-79 winter. The problem was that no-one had gritted the roads...

Because of a gritters' strike from 15-19 February 1979, which coincided with a bone-chilling cold spell and snow, roads in Sheffield were virtual 'no-go' areas.

Conditions throughout the UK were appalling and the Government appointed Dennis Howell as the 'Snow Minister'. Presumably, the brief given to this 'weather general' was to seek the help of another general referred to by forecasters when it was turning milder, General Thaw.

He flew into Sheffield, by helicopter, on 16 February and described the scene from the air as 'desolate'. His offer to send in the Army to solve the city's problems was politely declined.

The winter of 1979 and 20-year-old David Stuart carries supplies of water to the frozen Dyson Cote Farm, Oxspring, Penistone.

Snow hangs from the trees on Houndkirk Road, Ringinglow, Sheffield, on New Year's Day 1979.

Fun for some at Bingham Park, Sheffield, on 1 January 1979.

Skis on and almost ready for the off on the slopes of Ringinglow in 1979 are Derek Holdsworth of Dore, Sheffield (nearest camera) and John Duffy, of Chelsea Road, Brincliffe, Sheffield.

It's a long, cold wait for commuters in February 1979, as they queue for taxis home in Fitzalan Square during the gritters' strike. All the city's buses had stopped running because of the state of the roads throughout the city.

Greenmoor, Sheffield, fails to live up to its name on 25 February 1975.

With the lake at Longshaw frozen solid after a week of bitter weather in December 1973, it was an opportunity for mums, dads and children to stage an impromptu game of ice hockey before going home for Sunday lunch.

Three young members of Hallamshire Ski Club take the easy way up the steep slopes of Sheffield's Meersbrook Park in March 1970, after a ski-tow winch had been installed.

Paradise Square, Sheffield, is usually full of cars – except on 20 January 1979, when heavy snow made access impossible.

The outskirts of Sheffield were in the icy grip of winter on 1 November 1975. Seen here is the snow affected Hathersage Road running past the Blacka Plantation.

Volunteer fans help to clear snow from Sheffield United's Bramall Lane ground in February 1979.

Gales brought down a gable end wall onto a line of cars at an Attercliffe Common car sales site in January 1976.

This was the seafront sight greeting Sheffielders spending a week-end in Scarborough in May 1973. Gales whipped up heavy seas, causing damage to the sea wall and paving.

A dramatic picture at Tinsley, Sheffield, in May 1979, as water cascades from the top deck of the M1 after heavy rain.

Heavy flooding under the railway bridge at Fife Street, Wincobank, Sheffield, in February 1977, after Blackburn Brook had burst its banks.

After flood water swept into homes on Holgate
Avenue, Parson Cross, Sheffield, in May 1979,
Norman Knight (left) and his brother in law Ray
Jackson faced a big clean-up.

The weir on the River Don at Lady's Bridge,
Sheffield, has almost disappeared as water pours
over it following torrential rain in February 1977.

The Sheffield to
Rotherham road looks
more like a river in
April 1970.

Sheaf Gardens, Sheffield,
was an awful mess after
flooding in July 1973, so
the locals turned out to
wash away the mud.

Total chaos in Sheffield after the July 1973, downpour. A number 60 bus heading for Nether Green is in trouble, as is the car next to it.

Shoppers dodge flood water on Manchester Road, Stocksbridge, Sheffield, in December 1978.

A carpet of leaves covers Sheffield Cathedral forecourt on a rainy Autumn day in October 1974.

Hot sunshine in June 1978, brought out the crowds in Sheffield and this was the scene outside the Dove and Rainbow pub in the city centre.

Sunshine, a paddling pool, shrieks of delight… Millhouses Park, Sheffield, on a warm afternoon in June 1973.

That's one way of keeping cool on a hot day! Youngsters on a play scheme at Parson Cross Park in August 1975, get a welcome shower from park supervisor Jack Gray.

Industry

Trouble And Strife, The Three- Day Week And No Television After 10.30pm

The 70s was a much troubled decade industrially with overtime bans, go slows, work to rules and strikes causing widespread disruption in most areas of public life.

In the first quarter of 1971, days lost by strikes were four times that of the same quarter the year before.

Possibly the worst misery came in the winter of 1973-74 when Edward Heath's Conservative government found itself at loggerheads with the unions.

On top of an oil crisis in the Middle East, there were disputes involving power workers and railway staff as well as the mineworkers who started an overtime ban in November 1973 and then a strike in February 1974.

To save energy, the Government put industry on a three-day week and other restrictive measures included a top speed of 50mph on the roads, heating restrictions in factories, no television after 10.30pm and a ban on illuminated advertising signs.

Food shops were exempt from the three-day week and one enterprising hairdresser sidestepped the restrictions by offering baked beans at 75p per tin with a free shampoo and set thrown in!

It was a grim winter and it led to the downfall of the Heath government. The Prime Minister called an election on the issue of 'who is running the country, the Government or the unions?' and Harold Wilson took power at the head of a minority Labour Government.

The mineworkers, who eventually went back to work on 11 March, were also on strike, for seven weeks, in the winter of 1972.

They walked out in January, for the first time in about 50 years, demanding an 11 per cent increase in basic wages.

There was strife on many fronts during the decade. In January 1970, schoolchildren in Sheffield had a week's holiday because of strike action by teachers and, in January 1971, thousands of local trade union members stopped work in protest at the Government's Industrial Relations Bill.

In 1974, Sheffield resembled a huge rubbish dump during a five-week strike by supervisory foremen working for the Cleansing Department. When it finished, there were 15,000 tons of rubbish to clear up.

And in 1978, refuse collectors refused to take any rubbish that wasn't in bins and the ban lasted for six months.

Bus crews also took action several times during the decade, causing problems on the roads. In February 1979, the city's roads network virtually closed down when road gritters came out on strike during a bitterly cold spell with temperatures barely climbing above freezing point.

1972 and Arthur
Scargill addresses the
crowd at a miners
and engineers
demonstration.

Derbyshire miners on the
march in February 1972.
A band can be seen playing on
the far left of the picture, near
the NUPE Clay Cross Branch
banner.

Pickets outside the premises of Barnsley coal merchants, Freemans, of Pontefract Road, in January 1972.

Miners' wives picking coal at Clay Cross in February 1972.

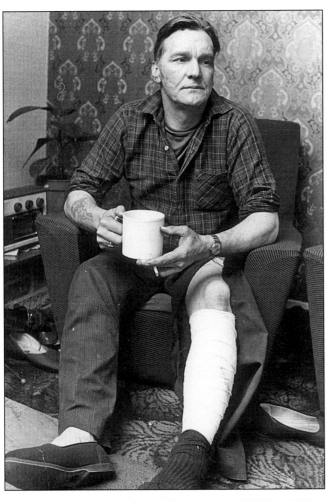

George Shaw, of Wombwell, Barnsley, relaxes at home with a cup of tea after receiving hospital treatment for an injured leg. He was involved in an accident with a lorry on the picket lines outside the Coalite plant at Grimethorpe in January 1972.

Miners collecting coal for pensioners during the 1974 dispute.

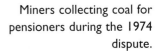

Miners leave the pit head at Manvers Main Colliery after their last shift before the start of the 1974 strike.

Pickets huddle underneath their makeshift shelter at Birley East pit, Woodhouse, Sheffield, in February 1974.

Vast crowds attended a miners support rally outside Sheffield City Hall in February 1974.

Saturday afternoon in Fargate, Sheffield, in December 1973, and mineworkers from Hickleton, Doncaster, drum up support from the public.

Yorkshire NUM president Arthur Scargill pictured in January 1974, with one of the posters sent to NUM branches and collieries throughout the Yorkshire coalfield.

X-Ray staff at Sheffield's Northern General Hospital hand out leaflets to passers-by after coming out on strike in August 1974.

Bassetlaw MP Joe Ashton addresses a meeting of hospital workers at a meeting in the Cattle Market at Worksop in March 1973. One banner proclaims that a wage of £16 a week is a crime.

Striking firemen from all over the country delivered a 500,000-signature petition supporting their case for more pay to the Prime Minister in November 1977. In this picture, Arthur Scargill visits a local picket line in Sheffield to offer moral support.

Firemen picketing Sheffield's Division Street Fire Station in November 1977, during the national strike.

The Army were on standby during the firemen's dispute in November 1977, and members of 30 Battery, 16 Air Defence Royal Artillery are seen relaxing at the Manor TA Centre, Sheffield, in November 1977.

Rubbish builds up in a Sheffield subway in June 1974, during a five-week dustbin strike.

When Sheffield Cleansing Department staff went on strike in October 1970, a group of teenagers took it upon themselves to clear rubbish from Sheffield's Castle Square. But it led to a confrontation with union representatives.

At the height of the 1974 strike, third year and sixth form pupils from Sheffield's Ashleigh Comprehensive School volunteered to collect rubbish from The Moor.

Sheffield binmen went on strike in June 1978, after refusing to collect any rubbish that was not contained in bins. This picture shows piles of smelling rubbish stored in sacks in one of the garages underneath Hyde Park Flats.

The two-week strike was over by 7 July 1978, and Sheffield's dustmen faced a mountain of refuse. This crew are pictured hard at work on the Manor Estate, Sheffield.

Striking social workers on the steps of Sheffield Town Hall in March 1979. One banner carries the message 'Dedication doesn't pay the bills. Pay social workers the rate for the job.' Another says: 'Support social workers today for a better service tomorrow.'

Post office workers march through the city centre on their way to a strike meeting at Sheffield City Hall in January 1971.

Students on the march as they leave Sheffield Education Offices in March 1977 after a sit-in.

A busmen's meeting in Rotherham meant a long wait for travellers wanting to get back to Sheffield in September 1970.

A queue for taxis in Fitzalan Square, Sheffield, on 26 September 1974, after a bus stoppage had hit Sheffield.

Lots of buses at Sheffield's Pond Street in September 1974, but no drivers because of a stoppage.

Queues build up at a bus stop in High Street, Sheffield, in 1977.

Schooldays

Education All At Sea For Lucky Pupils

For the children lucky enough to be on them, educational cruises in the 70s were a mind-stretching experience, combining learning with the delights of a holiday in far-flung places.

Pupils from several Sheffield schools boarded the SS Uganda in February, 1976, and these pictures capture some of the flavour of the trip. They were taken by Frank Travers, a photographer on the former *Morning Telegraph* at the time. Swapping the winter streets of Sheffield for a sunshine life on the ocean waves must have been arduous…

Children from Gleadless Valley School, Sheffield, are shown Turkish cigarette pipes by a street vendor in Istanbul.

Sheffield Tapton School pupils inspect necklaces in Istanbul.

All at sea are children from Rowlinson School, Sheffield, pictured on the bridge with Navigating Cadet Nicholas McGregor.

Not many miserable faces here, even though this group was involved in a study session on board.

Sheffield Colley School pupils pictured in Dubrovnik with a Yugoslav lady in national dress.

Girls from King Ecgbert School, Sheffield, pose for not one but two photographers!

A party from Ashleigh School, Sheffield, in front of the Temple of Memmus in the ruins of Ephesus.

Teacher Terry Stapley, from Carter Lodge School, Sheffield, passes on a few photographic tips to (from left) pupils Glyn Lower, David Ellen, Stephenson Davidson and Alan Myers.

Meanwhile, Back At Home...

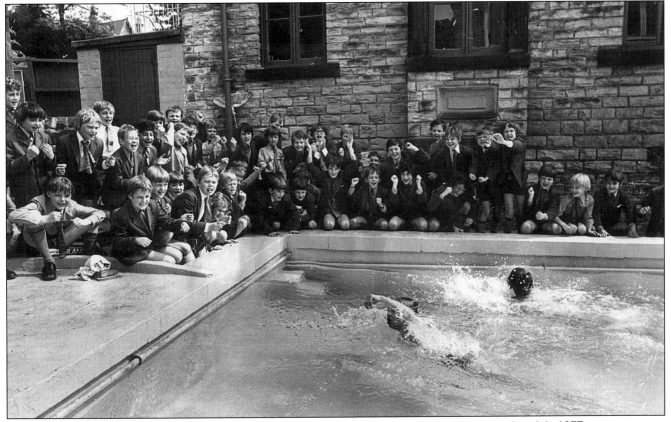

Boys from Birkdale Preparatory School, Sheffield, cheer on their mates at a school swimming gala in July 1977.

Ten young boys and girls from Sheffield's Brightside Primary School wrote to *The Star* in January 1970, protesting about vandalism to the tree saplings they had planted. They are (left to right), front, Beverley Foster, Gillian Cliff; second row, Patricia Turner, Angela Simons, David Unwin, Mark Taff; third row, Harold Longman, Gary McLachlan, Craig Hawksworth and Neil Gretton.

Pupils from Firth Park School, Sheffield, pictured on the school steps in July 1973.

Parents were invited along to St Paul's School, Granville Road, Sheffield, in October 1970, to see how 'modern' science lessons were taught. Mary Nestor, aged 13 (left) holds burning magnesium to demonstrate the effects of heat. Helping with the experiment (right) is Carmel Nichols (12).

April 1970, and let's hope these children from Sheffield's Hadfield House School managed to pull up before reaching the photographer.

Dronfield Woodhouse William Levick Primary School headmaster George Hickling pictured with some of his pupils in October, 1975.

Sister Nativity and her class at St Patrick's RC Junior and Infants School, Sheffield Lane Top, in July 1973.

Pupil Barbara Wright tries out a new hearing aid device at Sheffield's Maud Maxfield School for the Deaf in May 1978. Helping her is Miss Wendy Suttle.

Television personality John Junkin pictured at St John's C of E School, Sheffield, in 1975.

Pupils from Sheffield's Park High School converted a former 100-ton coal barge into a floating residential classroom in 1970 and launched it on the canal at Attercliffe, Sheffield. From the left are: Science master Mr D. Cliffe, Mr R. Smith, Head of Crafts, and Fourth Year boys Robert Hughes, Garry Mitchell, Paul Harris, David Henshaw, Martyn Howard, Paul James and David Rothwell.

Sheffield Boys Independent Grammar School held a service of thanksgiving at Sheffield Cathedral in January 1978. Seated from the left are: Dr J. Colin Davies, consultant principal and co-founder of the school; Dr T.A. James, senior school headmaster; Dr J.M. Whittaker, former Vice-Chancellor, University of Sheffield, and official school visitor; Mr Bernard Ambler, co-founder; the Revd Canon, Prof James Atkinson, member of the school court; pupil Charles Hunt, aged 13; the Very Revd W. Frank Curtis, Provost of Sheffield. Looking on are members of the school's staff.

Eckington's new primary school opened in March 1975, and it's an exciting time for these youngsters as they wait for lessons to start.

Young pupils of Sheffield's Lowfield Junior School campaigned to save the White House, on Bramall Lane, Sheffield, from demolition in February 1973. They are pictured here with teacher Dorothy Dromgoole and head Chris Rosling.

Sheffield's Limpsfield Middle School opened its new library in January 1977.

Grub's up! Sheffield's Ashleigh School in September 1971 where self-service lunches were on the menu.

Big hearted children from Beck School, Sheffield, staged a Christmas concert in December 1979, and used the proceeds to buy tins of food for the Telegraph and Star Old Folks Fund Christmas distribution to old and needy people.

Pupils at Ashleigh School, Sheffield, helped pack Christmas parcels for the Telegraph and Star Old Folks Fund distribution scheme in 1975.

Christmas 1978 and pictured with more than 1,000 tins of food given by pupils and parents from King Edward Lower School, Darwin Lane, Crosspool, for the Telegraph and Star Old Folks Fund Christmas parcels are (from left) Gabrielle Pearson, aged 11, Linda Williams, 14, and Paul Beresford, 12.

Thumbs up from children of the Beighton, Sheffield, Play Scheme as they leave Sheffield Canal Basin on board Princess Katharine for a trip down the South Yorkshire Navigation Canal on 13 August 1979.

Children playing happily at Sheffield Abbeydale Primary School in February 1975 while their parents were attending an English course for Chinese restaurant workers.

The Shepherds' Wheel in Whiteley Woods, Sheffield, was working for the first time in 40 years on 18 May 1979, to mark International Museums Day and children from Hucklow Middle School, Firth Park, Sheffield, went along to sketch the buildings.

That's Entertainment!

Fiesta Time As Sheffield's Nightlife Takes Off

Sheffield's nightlife was starting to take off as never before as the 70s dawned.

The Bailey Organisation's Cavendish Club on Queen Street, the city's first real night club, had opened in 1967 with singer Kathy Kirby providing the cabaret for the opening week and two months later it had a staggering 20,000 members and a waiting list.

By August 1970 it had a rival – the 1,300 – seater Fiesta Club on Arundel Gate. The Shadows played there on opening night to be followed by Matt Monro, Clodagh Rodgers, the Rockin Berries, Tommy Cooper and many more national and international superstars.

After so long without, Sheffield now had two sophisticated nightspots. The city's Lord Mayor, Alderman Sidney Dyson, performed the opening ceremony at the Fiesta and described it as a momentous occasion.

'Sheffield needs to look forward to the future as far as leisure for its citizens is concerned and we are indebted to the enterprise of the Lipthorpe brothers in choosing Sheffield for a leisure centre.'

Keith Lipthorpe, chairman and joint managing director of the Fiesta with brother Jim, said that Sheffield was found to be the best site for a new £500,000 night club after a survey of cities in the north.

In 1973, Keith made a determined bid to land Elvis Presley for the Fiesta but the move failed and the legendary Elvis never came to England.

Not all Sheffielders, however, were ready for the Fiesta, or rather its prices. In 1975 door staff started searching the handbags of women customers to stop them smuggling in their own drink.

The girls and their partners had been bringing in their own spirit miniatures to beat prices and delays in getting served.

The Fiesta Club was officially opened in August 1970 by the Lord Mayor and Lady Mayoress of Sheffield, Alderman and Mrs Sidney Dyson, who were given a tour of the premises by Keith Lipthorpe, chairman and joint managing director of the club.

A crowded dance floor at the Fiesta.

The Shadows provided the cabaret at the Fiesta's opening night.

The main entrance to the Fiesta Club. The Barron Knights were appearing in cabaret when this picture was taken in 1976. Note the poster advertising the Three Degrees.

Baileys Club, on Queen Street, Sheffield, was another popular haunt for 1970s nightlifers. This picture was taken in 1977.

Hysteria As Bay City Rollers Hit Town

Sheffield City Hall had never known a night quite like it...

They called it Rollermania and it resulted in 12 fans of the Scottish group Bay City Rollers receiving hospital treatment and another 100 needing attention from overworked first-aid staff during a concert in May 1975.

City Hall corridors became casualty stations as hysterical fans, overcome by the occasion, fainted and had to be carried out. Some had leg and rib injuries caused by the crush.

There were reports of one fan fainting three times – and each time she went back into the concert hall after treatment!

Rollermania comes to town as Bay City Rollers fans are treated in the City Hall corridors.

And here's the reason for all the hysteria – the Bay City Rollers on stage in May 1975.

The boys were back in Sheffield in September the following year and these two pictures show sections of the group's tartan-clad crowd of dedicated followers.

It's nearly all too much for these two fans...

Dedicated or what? Fans Sandra Furniss (left) and Carole Fisher show off their Rollermania memorabilia in April 1976.

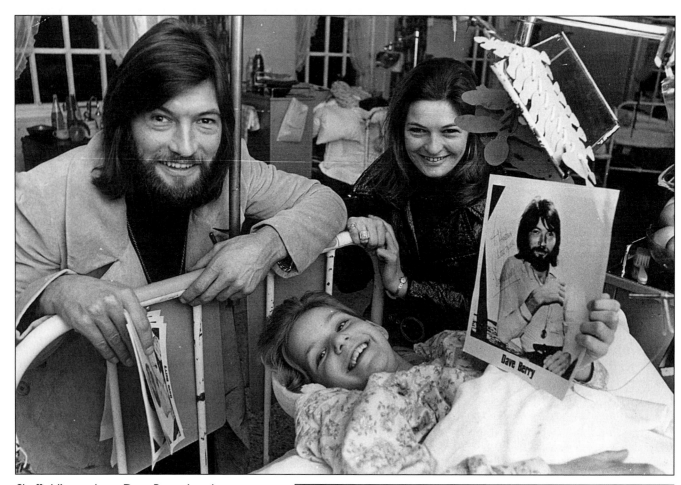

Sheffield's pop hero Dave Berry, hugely popular in the 60s and 70s and still going strong in 2002, has always been a fine ambassador for the city. In December 1970, he gave seven-year-old Heather Butler, of Gleadless Road, Sheffield, the surprise of her life by visiting her at King Edward VII Hospital. Heather, a distant relative of the pop singer and an ardent fan, had asked for some photographs of the star so Dave, accompanied by his sister Julie, decided to deliver them personally. He also gave signed photographs to other patients at the hospital.

Another Sheffield pop star, Tony Christie, also enjoyed cheering up patients at our local hospitals and here he is on a visit to the Children's Hospital in October 1977.

Although not local, Roy Castle rarely missed an opportunity to brighten the lives of youngsters when he was in our area. This little lad in Sheffield Children's Hospital in February 1979, looks as pleased as punch to see him.

Sheffield's own Marti Caine was hitting the high spots in the 70s, starring in her own television series and appearing in cabaret at the MGM Grand Hotel in Las Vegas where she won rave reviews from international stars such as Vic Damone and Glen Campbell. She also enchanted Liberace with her style and performance. This picture shows her leaving for Las Vegas with her then husband Malcolm.

Marti in 1979. She died tragically young in 1995 and her death was a sad loss to Sheffield.

Former Shirecliffe, Sheffield, schoolgirl Dianne Lee and blind pianist and singer Lennie Peters were the first group since the Beatles to have a number one single, *Welcome Home*, and a number one album at the same time in the 70s. Hugely successful, they appeared at Blackpool's North Pier for 22 consecutive weeks. Lennie died in 1992.

South Yorkshire favourite Stan Richards joined the cast of *Emmerdale* in 1978 as the village odd job man. Seth Armstrong had arrived! Here he is pictured with Christie G. (Robin Hood) when he appeared as the Sheriff of Nottingham in *Babes In The Wood* at Sheffield's Fiesta Club in 1979.

Women's Circle – A Star Success Story Of The 70s

One of *The Star's* many success stories of the 70s was its Women's Circle section. As well as enjoying discounts and special offers on a wide range of products, members, who were all readers of the newspaper, enjoyed social get-togethers, days out and trips to the theatre.

The Circle even had its own choir, performing to a high standard at various venues throughout the region and beyond.

Lifelong friendships resulted from the Circle which, because of its many and varied interests and activities, had such a broad appeal.

Members of The Star Women's Circle filled the Fiesta Club to capacity on January 1971 and met The Bachelors who were topping the bill.

Another special night at the Fiesta Club, in June 1971, and lots of smiles from Circle members as they laughed along with Harry Secombe.

A Circle trip to see *Fiddler on the Roof* in London gave these members an opportunity to meet Alfie Bass, the star of the show.

Comedian Jimmy Tarbuck cuts the cake at a 1971 Women's Circle birthday celebration.

Christmas 1972 and the Women's Circle Choir is in fine voice at one of its regular concerts.

Fund-raising balls organised by the Sheffield Committee of the Variety Club of Great Britain were popular events in the 70s and this star-studded night at the Top Rank Suite in October 1972 was supported by celebrities Peter Cushing (of horror film fame), Madeline Smith and Bernard Lee (from the Bond films). There to welcome them was Variety Club hostess Kate Wallis.

Na then, mi owd flower! South Yorkshire comic Charlie Williams was at Lees Hall Golf Club, Sheffield, in May 1978 for a Pro Am golf tournament. With him on the first tee are (from left): Lees Hall captain Paul Swindon, vice-captain Barry Wright and Roger Holland.

Sheffield's own Reginald Dixon, famous Blackpool Tower organist, was back in the city in August 1975 to play for members of the Sheffield Theatre Organ Society. He is pictured here with the Lord Mayor of Sheffield, Alderman Reg Munn.

The television cameras roll for the Lord Mayor and Lady Mayoress of Sheffield, Alderman and Mrs Harold Hebblethwaite, after the opening of Sheffield's Crucible Theatre in November 1971.

The campaign to reopen Sheffield's splendid Lyceum Theatre was underway in the 70s but it was to be 1990 before it actually happened. Both these photographs were taken in 1975.

The threatened closure of Sheffield's Silver Blades Ice Rink led to these young skaters staging a protest in May 1970.

Sheffield has long been a stronghold for quality male voice choirs and on song in this 1978 picture are members of North Anston MVC.

Bolsterstone Male Voice Choir show off their trophies in 1978. At the time of writing (2002) they are British champions and fine ambassadors for Sheffield.

Oh brother! The seven singing Pearsons from the Stocksbridge area were popular barbershop-style performers in the 70s. So meet (from the left) Geoff, Roger, John, Graham, Eric, Alf and Raymond. All of them apart from Geoff are current members of Bolsterstone Male Voice Choir.

Sheffield's Beauchief Singers who appeared in concert at the City Hall in 1971.

Looking outstandingly smart and ready to give it some oompha in 1976 were members of the Dronfield Band.

Top Stars Cut Their Teeth At Local Workingmen's Clubs

Workingmen's Clubs have long been a source of first-class entertainment in the Sheffield area with many of them providing 'turns' several nights a week and particularly at weekends.

Some of the top stars of the 70s cut their teeth at local workingmen's clubs and rated them as ideal preparation for the 'big time'.

This 1977 picture was taken at Sheffield Woodseats Club and the concert room is almost full.

Crookes WMC in March 1977, and not a miserable face in sight!

A quiet drink and chat for members of Hackenthorpe Social Club, Sheffield, in May 1977.

Lights Go Out
At Attercliffe Pavilion

For years the haunt of cinema buffs, courting couples, kids with stars in their eyes and those just wanting to escape the pressures of life for a night, the Pavilion Cinema at Attercliffe, Sheffield, finally closed its doors in 1979.

It had opened in 1915 but, like many picture houses, became a bingo hall in 1970. But, unlike many others, it reverted back to a cinema, specialising in Asian films, after only a few weeks and managed to hold on until the end of the decade.

We also lost the Odeon on Flat Street, Sheffield, in June 1971, and the Vogue, Sheffield Lane Top, in October 1975.

The Studio 7 on the Wicker (known as the Wicker from its opening in 1920 until it was badly damaged by fire in 1967 and rebuilt and re-opened as the Studio 7 in 1968) closed in January 1973 but then resurfaced as three cinemas, Studios 5, 6 and 7, a year and a half later.

It finally closed in August 1987.

The screen says it all. It's the end for the Vogue Cinema, Sheffield Lane Top, in October 1975. Pictured left to right on the sad day are manager Steve Kay and staff Jack Ward and Jean Haythorne.

The Pavilion Cinema, Attercliffe, in 1971 when it was showing Asian films.

The Odeon, Flat Street, in February 1971, about four months before it closed.

Fashion and Beauty

Hotpants Really Are The Limit, Says Princess Anne

HOTPANTS, flares, platform shoes, cheesecloth shirts – the 70s was certainly not a dull decade for fashion but not all of it found favour, particularly in Royal circles.

Princess Anne, for instance, was far from amused by hotpants, declaring regally: 'Hot pants are the limit. People complain you are not with it, but there are certain things I will not do.'

And what grandma said when punk fashion came along is just not printable.

A shop catering specifically for punk rockers in the Sheffield region opened on Ecclesall Road, Sheffield, in 1977 and was the first of its kind in the north of England. Owners Michael Peters (standing) and Graham Bull (kneeling) are pictured looking after customers Beverley Sales and Kathleen Furniss, both aged 18.

Teddy Boys were alive and well in 1974 as this picture taken outside Sheffield's Barley Corn Hotel shows.

All in a good cause – Teddy Boys from the Parson Cross area of Sheffield held a sponsored rock 'n' roll night at St Bernard's Church Hall, Southey Hill, Sheffield, to raise money for St Cecilia's Church Boiler Fund. Pictured left to right standing are: Roger Peacock, aged 14, Andrew Ledger, 14, Paul Wilson, 15, Cameron Whiteley, 14, Tony Brookes, 14. In front is 16-year-old Martin Ledger.

The king is dead, long live the king. After Elvis Presley's death in 1977, these Sheffield fans laid a wreath in the city centre as a tribute to their idol.

Miss Sheffield Pam Wood cuts a dash in hotpants. She was runner-up in the Miss England competition in 1971.

Pam again, this time modelling a white, soft-grained leather wedding outfit which was the highlight of a local Suede and Leather fashion show in 1971.

Children's fashion in Sheffield in 1974.

1970 and the midi skirt turns a head or two in the middle of Sheffield.

Sheffield's Christine Owen models a 70s dress. A former Miss UK, Christine was also a hostess on the popular *Sale of the Century* television programme.

What the well-dressed Sheffield man about town was wearing in 1973 when suits with waistcoats were in fashion.

The Star's photographer went out into the countryside around Sheffield in 1970 for this stylish picture of fashionable evening wear.

In the days before the coal industry started to decline, contestants representing coalfields from all over the country competed in the national coal queen competition. The 1971 final was held in Doncaster and our local representative, Julia Baker, is seen sitting in front of the other competitors.

Miss United Kingdom, Madeleine Stringer, was a visitor to Debenhams store, Sheffield, in 1977.

Days Out in the 70s

Taking A Break From The Stresses And Strains

GOING out for the day in the 70s was often a welcome release from the stress and frustration caused by the decade's industrial troubles.

But there again, Sheffielders always have known how to enjoy themselves as this selection of pictures shows...

The message couldn't be clearer – Sheffield Spectacular starts on Saturday! Touring the city centre in June 1975 were (left to right) June Lindley, Kathleen Quayle and Sue Higgins.

Riding alongside the floats in the Sheffield Spectacular Lord Mayor's Parade of 1975 were these 33 ladies pictured outside T.W. Ward's Albion Works, Sheffield.

Flag waving children and mums and dads watch the 1975 Lord Mayor's Parade go by.

A Great Sheffield Race was staged in conjunction with the 1975 Sheffield Spectacular and these are some of the competitors waiting for the action to start.

Student Fun Raised Vital Charity Money

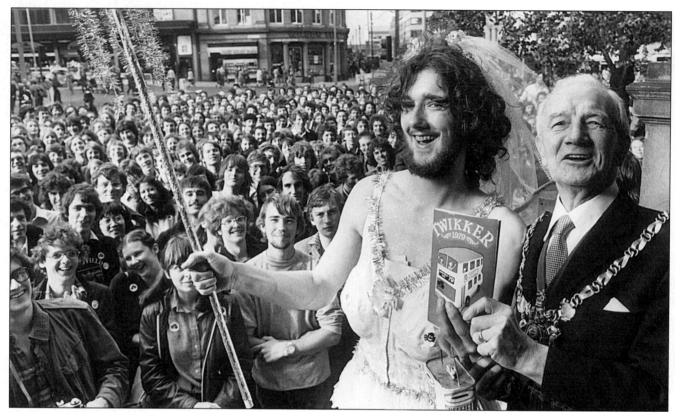

Thousands of Sheffielders turned out in the 70s to watch the zany antics of students taking part in the annual Rag Parade. In this 1979 picture, Rag fairy David Richards sells a copy of the *Twikker* rag magazine to the Lord Mayor of Sheffield, Councillor George Armitage.

Armed with collecting boxes and copies of the *Twikker* magazine, Sheffield University students besiege the city centre in October 1977. Their efforts were much appreciated by local charities who benefited from the fund-raising.

The 1979 Rag Parade weaves its way down Church Street, Sheffield, and into High Street.

According to the notice, the last wife auction to be held in Sheffield before this 1972 Rag Day event on Fargate, Sheffield, was in 1796!

Monster fun in the 1970 Rag Parade.

'Ascension Day' outside Sheffield Cathedral in 1971 as students billed as the Magnificent Madmen take to the air... just.

Spectators line the banks of the River Don in Sheffield to watch the 1970 Rag Day raft race.

Huge crowds lap up the sunshine at Sheffield Show in 1979.

Children enjoy a police dog demonstration at Arbourthorne School, Sheffield, in November 1970. The little lad on the right got into the swing of things by borrowing a policeman's helmet.

All the fun of the fair at the 1974 Sheffield Show held at Hillsborough Park.

The Army stand at the 1974 Sheffield Show attracted this group of inquisitive youngsters.

Not an adult in sight as the crowds gather for an open air rock concert at Sheffield's Weston Park in July 1979.

Members of Sheffield's Gingerbread Club get together for a day of fun at Hillsborough Park, Sheffield, in May 1975.

After the opening of their new pavilion in April 1972, members of the Sheffield Whiteley Woods Bowls Club were soon in action on the green.

Members of Sheffield's Firth Park Bowling Club admire the Spring blooms as they make their way to the greens in March 1972.

Young anglers from Sheffield's Rowlinson Comprehensive School entered the national schoolboys angling championships in 1976 and here they receive expert tuition at Graves Park from Gladys Evans who at that time was the only female coach in the country.

Sheffield's Firth Park held its centenary celebrations in August 1975 and this streamlined exhibit – it looks like a racing craft – received plenty of attention.

Not the best way of spending a day out in the park! Workmen use a suction tanker to remove oil from the Porter Brook in Endcliffe Park, Sheffield, after it had become polluted. Ducks affected by the oil made a good recovery after bring 'dressed' in special coats made from discarded tights.

Not everyone's idea of a good day out but all credit to this charity-minded quartet who were pushing a pram all the way from Lands End to Sheffield in 1977 to raise money for the Telegraph and Star Old Folk's Fund.

The annual Christian gathering at Cliff College, Derbyshire, attracted hundreds of churchgoers from the Sheffield area every year. Lunch is about to be served at the 1971 event.

Worshippers celebrate at the 1975 Cliff College gathering.

The July 1976 Sheffield Pageant drew thousands of people into the city centre and these young Vikings appear to be on the verge of doing something very nasty indeed to the photographer!

This delightful group of Anglo-Saxons –all Sheffield Girl Guides – wait patiently for the 1976 Sheffield Pageant to move off.

Six-year-old Claire Kingham, of Grenoside, Sheffield, doesn't look at all amused by these cavemen. Hardly surprising. You go along to the Sheffield Pageant for a pleasant day out and this is what confronts you...

This must be a 'first' – Teddy Boys chatting to Roman soldiers at the 1976 Sheffield Pageant and no doubt telling them they are a bit behind in the fashion stakes.

The Sheffield Pageant parade passes Sheffield Town Hall in 1976.

A band leads the hymn singing at the 1976 Whit Sing in Firth Park, Sheffield.

Paradise Square, Sheffield, where John Wesley preached, was the setting for this torchlight carol service at Christmas 1979.

Splashing out for charity at Glossop Road Baths in 1971 were these sponsored swimmers raising cash for the National Trust for the Welfare of the Elderly.

After officially opening Sheaf Valley Baths in November 1972, Rolf Harris was happy to splash about – with paint!

A group of senior citizens receive swimming tuition from Rose Gore at Sheaf Valley Baths in September 1976.

Members of Chapeltown, Sheffield, Round Table clowning about at an Arts Ball in 1976.

Yard of Ale competitions would no doubt be frowned on now as would any drinking contest but they were very popular in the 70s. The idea was to drink the whole lot in one attempt. Barman Tom Redfearn tried, and failed, at a 1971 Sheffield Norfolk Park Tenants Association social evening.

This young magpie's idea of a good time in 1971 was to call at Grenoside Working Men's Club, Sheffield, every night for a drink of beer, a packet of crisps and then bed down at the side of an electric heater. Sounds almost human!

Royal Visits

Queen Goes Walkabout In Fargate

SHEFFIELD certainly couldn't complain about a lack of royal visitors during the 70s.

The Queen came in 1975 and thrilled the vast crowds by going walkabout in Fargate, later opening the new South Yorkshire Police headquarters on Snig Hill.

She returned two years later during her Silver Jubilee Year when Sheffield celebrated with 11 days of special events.

Princess Anne opened Weston Park Hospital in July 1970, and Prince Charles was here to give a Royal blessing to the Hallamshire Hospital when it opened in 1979.

Prince Charles was also in the city in 1975, principally to visit the Maud Maxfield School for hard of hearing children.

And in 1976, Princess Margaret toured Sheffield Children's Hospital when it celebrated its centenary.

A close-up view of the Queen for these smiling Sheffielders when she went walkabout in Fargate during her visit to the city in 1975.

Joyous crowds on Fargate in 1975 as the Lord Mayor, Councillor Albert Richardson, walks proudly at the Queen's side.

A general view of Fargate in 1975 just before the Queen started her walkabout.

The Queen's Silver Jubilee Visit In 1977

July 12, 1977, was a big day for Coun Mrs Winifred Golding, the Lord Mayor of Sheffield, when she received the Queen during her Silver Jubilee visit to Hillsborough Park.

Uniformed organisations spell out the clearest of welcomes to the Queen during her 1977 Silver Jubilee visit to Sheffield.

It's not every day the Queen passes by so these pupils from Sheffield's Foxhill Middle School had good reason to get excited.

Princess Anne At Weston Park Hospital

Princess Anne talks to one of the sisters during her visit to Weston Park Hospital in 1970.

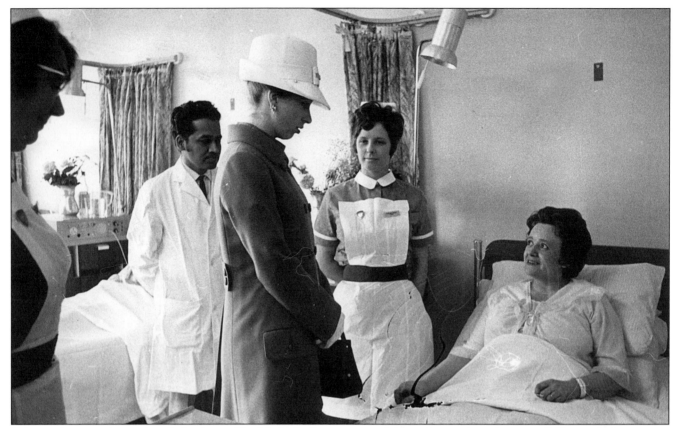

Princess Anne made a point of chatting to Mrs Marjorie Garrett, one of the patients, when she toured Weston Park Hospital.

Prince Charles Tours Maud Maxfield School

These children look spellbound as Prince Charles puts over a point.

Prince Charles wonders what he should say to it as Dr John Worrall, chairman of the Maud Maxfield School governors, shows him a guinea pig, one of the pets kept by children at the school.

Six-year-old Peter Beer, of Fairfax Road, Manor, Sheffield, is introduced to Princess Margaret during her tour of Sheffield Children's Hospital in July 1976.

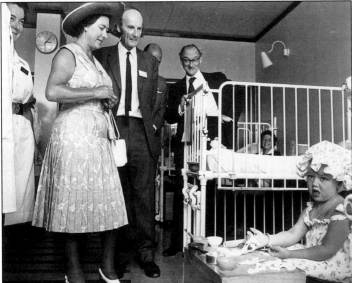

Fit for a Princess! Little Tara Wilson, aged four, is busy cooking as Princess Margaret stops to watch her cutting out jam tarts from a layer of pastry.

Children's Hospital Centenary Celebrations

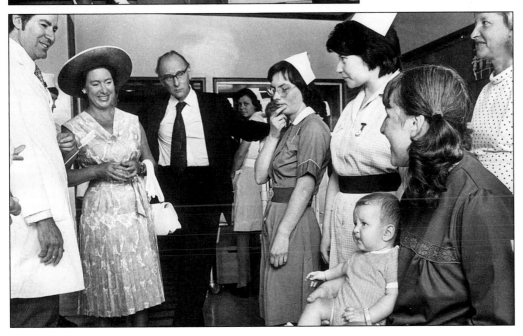

Six months old Lloyd Clayton sits on his mum, Pamela's, knee, and has no idea that a very special royal visitor has come to see him.

Royal Blessing For Hallamshire Hospital

1979 and Prince Charles jokes with the tea ladies at the Royal Hallamshire Hospital. He asked them if they put bromide in patients' tea!

Medical staff welcome Prince Charles to the Royal Hallamshire Hospital.

Smiles all round as Prince Charles talks to staff in the coffee lounge.

Pupils from Crookes Endowed School, Sheffield, waved a welcome to Prince Charles when he arrived at Hayward House in Redcar Road, Sheffield, during his 1979 visit.

Tragedies and Dramas

Disasters Devastate Our Mining Communities

Our region suffered two dreadful mining accidents in the Seventies, sending shock waves through an industry which has known more than its fair share of disasters over the years.

It is hard to comprehend the intense grief felt by mining families whenever tragedy strikes. At times of such sadness, mining communities somehow find a precious kind of collective strength and unity to help console stricken families and share in their sense of loss.

A cage carrying miners to the bottom of the 440 yards deep Shonkey shaft at Markham Colliery south of Sheffield ran out of control in July 1973, killing 14 men and injuring 16 others.

In June 1975, five miners lost their lives when an explosion ripped through a virgin seam 1,200ft underground at Houghton Main Colliery, Barnsley. The men were preparing a new face for coal production when the accident happened.

The mining industry lost one of its staunchest local champions in 1979 when Tom Swain, Labour MP for North East Derbyshire and a former chairman of the Miners Group of MPs in the Commons, died following a collision between his mini and a lorry while out on a shopping trip at Staveley.

Mick McGahey, vice-president of the National Union of Mineworkers, said in a tribute that Tom had typified all that was best in the British Labour Movement and epitomised all that was best in the NUM.

The anguish is etched on the faces of miners as they bring out the dead and injured from Markham Colliery in 1973.

A pitiful scene at one of the funerals which followed the Markham tragedy.

The grim scene at Houghton Main Colliery, Barnsley, after the explosion in June 1975.

A group of women anxiously await news at the pithead after the Houghton Main disaster.

Arthur Scargill, president of the Yorkshire NUM and Government Energy Secretary Anthony Wedgwood Benn at the scene of the Houghton Main tragedy.

MP Tom Swain who was tragically killed in a road accident while out on a shopping trip in 1979. His white mini was badly damaged in a collision with a lorry.

Six Die In Sheffield Gas Works Blast

An explosion at a gas works in the middle of Sheffield in October 1973 killed three men working on modifications to an underground storage tank. Three others injured in the blast died later. The explosion, at the Effingham Street gasworks, left a crater described by rescuers as a 'hell hole' and scattered debris over an area of 200 square yards.

The 'hell-hole' crater left by the explosion at the Effingham Street gasworks.

Firemen at work on the edge of the crater. In the foreground, a sorry mess of cars wrecked by the blast.

The scene of devastation from the air. The crater can be clearly seen in the centre of the picture.

Further afield, two Sheffield women lost their lives and other local people were injured when the Summerland Fun Centre on the Isle of Man caught fire in August 73.

A spectacular car fire at the junction of Sharrow Lane and London Road, Sheffield, in 1975, after a Reliant three wheeler burst into flames.

Sheffield born soccer star and former England goalkeeper Gordon Banks survived a horror car crash in October 72. He was badly injured and lost the sight of his left eye but five weeks later posed for a photocall.

A few months after his car accident, brave Banks was back in our area playing in a match to raise money for the victims of the Markham Colliery disaster.

Roaming Lions Shot At Penistone

Drama near Penistone in 1975 after a lion and a lioness, Anthony and Cleopatra, escaped from their winter quarter pens at the Circus Americano and were shot by a farmer and a police marksman. They were free for two hours and were killed when they attacked a young calf in a farmer's field.

Subways were built for pedestrians so this car down the Fitzalan Square subway in 1979 created quite a stir.

Montgomery Hall Blaze Drama

A dramatic picture of firemen on ladders and hydraulic lifts fighting a serious fire at Sheffield's Montgomery Hall in May 1971.

The stage area was completely wrecked. Just about recognisable are a drum and a cymbal on the right of the stage.

The extent of the fire is seen in this shot of the circle and stage.

Sporting Sheffield

Football In The Doldrums –
Owls and Blades in Third Division

SHEFFIELD football in the 70s was a story of ups and downs and comings and goings…

And there were more downs than ups. At one stage towards the end of what was a generally disappointing decade for supporters on both sides of the city, both Wednesday and United were in the Third Division.

Yet it had all started so promisingly for the Blades. Promoted to the top flight under manager John Harris at the end of season 1970-71, they started the 1971-72 season with an incredible flourish, remaining unbeaten in their first ten matches, eight of which they won.

The run, which became the talking point of the country's football pundits, came to an end against Manchester United at Old Trafford in October when George Best scored one of his trademark goals.

United's success in the early 70s was one of the reasons why Bramall Lane, the Sheffield home of the Yorkshire cricket team as well as United, lost its cricket in 1973 and became a traditional four-sided football ground in 1976.

Bizarrely, that was also the year when the Blades, who should have been consolidating their Division One status, were relegated and by 1979 they had slipped into Division Three.

A little bit of football history was created on Boxing Day 1979 when a crowd of more than 49,000 for the Owls v Blades game at Hillsborough set a record for that division.

That local derby is still talked about today but only by Wednesdayites who dubbed their 4-0 victory 'The Boxing Day Massacre.'

History shows that the victory helped to give Wednesday lift-off and they were promoted to Division Two at the end of that season.

For United fans, the gloom deepened and relegation to Division Four followed in the 1980-81 season.

Wednesday had lost their place in the top flight as the 70s began and worse was to follow in 1975 when they dropped to the Third.

During the decade, Wednesday had five different managers and United four. Occupants of the Wednesday hot seat were Danny Williams, Derek Dooley, Steve Burtenshaw, Len Ashurst and Jack Charlton.

John Harris, Ken Furphy, Jimmy Sirrell and Harry Haslam were the men who tried to set Bramall Lane on fire but only Harris really succeeded.

Sheffield United soak up success in May 1971, after their promotion to Division One (now the Premiership). Players are reading a special promotion supplement produced by *The Star*.

A civic reception at the Town Hall in May 1971 gave the Lord Mayor, Alderman Sidney Dyson, a chance to show Sheffield United's players and officials a floral football display specially set up for the occasion. A flower head has been used for the ball.

United fanatic Mark Crampton, aged eight, was desperate to meet his heroes before he emigrated to Australia in May 1971. His wish was granted in abundance – 15 of them turned out to wish him bon voyage.

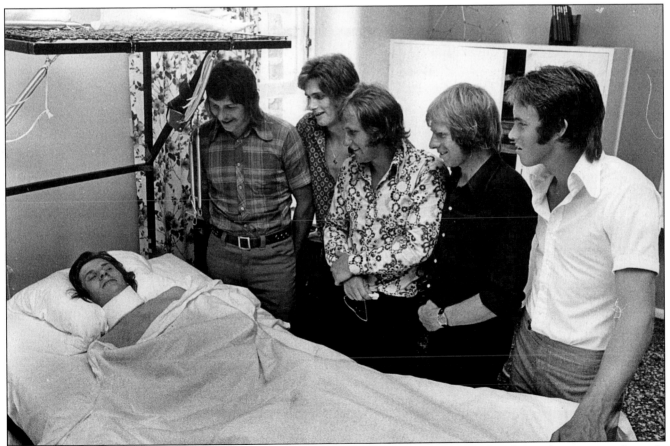

Sheffield United junior player Cliff Cartledge, in Sheffield's Lodge Moor Hospital in July 1972 with a neck injury, was cheered up by a visit from first team players Len Badger, Ted Hemsley, Geoff Salmons, Ian McKenzie and Tom McAllister.

United's conquering heroes pictured in July 1971, as they prepare for their return to the top flight. Back row (left to right): Alan Woodward, Colin Addison, Ted Hemsley, Len Badger, Tony Currie, John Hope, Geoff Salmons, John Flynn, Dave Powell, Frank Barlow, John Short (coach). Front row: Cec Coldwell (trainer), David Ford, Bill Dearden, Gil Reece, John Harris (manager), Eddie Colquhoun, Trevor Hockey and Stuart Scullion.

And this is what some of them looked like 15 years later at Tony Currie's testimonial match in 1986!

Brian Flynn puts a header between the posts to score United's second against Leicester City in April 1975.

United created something of a sensation in 1978 when they bought Argentinian international Alex Sabella from River Plate for a club record of £160,000. This picture shows him running out for his first match, against Leyton Orient, in August 1978.

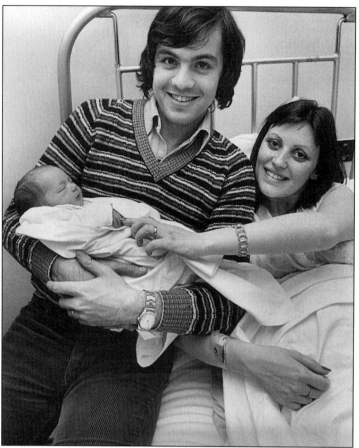

Proud dad Alex and his wife Vivianna with their new baby Vanessa Alexandra pictured at Sheffield's Jessop Hospital in October 1979.

They regularly played the 70s hit *You Can Do Magic* at Bramall Lane as a tribute to the superb skills of Tony Currie, affectionately known by the fans as TC. So imagine the heartbreak when he moved to Leeds in June 1976, for £275,000. This picture was taken just before the transfer.

Tony Currie was one of the football celebrities congratulating boxer John Conteh, British light heavyweight boxing champion, in 1974 after he had won the Yorkshire Television Sportsman of the Year award. Also in the picture (from left) are Sheffield Wednesday captain Ken Knighton and Sheffield United manager Ken Furphy.

Alan Woodward, prolific goalscorer and the perfect partner for Currie, was another United hero it was a privilege to watch in the 70s. The two of them are pictured outside Bramall Lane in February 1976.

Fellow players salute Alan Woodward at his benefit match in May 1974, and, in turn, Woody salutes the crowd.

Sheffield Wednesday's squad pictured before the start of the 1972-73 season at the end of which they finished tenth in the Second Division. Back row (left to right): Derek Dooley (manager), Peter Swan, Steve Downes, Dave Sunley, Alan Thompson, Peter Grummitt, Peter Rodrigues, Peter Springett, Colin Prophett, Sammy Todd, Paul Taylor, Jim Mullen, Ron Staniforth (coach). Front row: Mick Prendergast, Ken Burton, Jack Sinclair, Roy Coyle, Dave Clements, John Holsgrove, Brian Joicey, John Sissons, Tommy Craig, Eddie Prudham, Eric Potts, Willie Henderson.

Jack Charlton took over the Owls in 1977 and one of his acquisitions was the exciting Terry Curran from Southampton who went on to become a Hillsborough favourite. This pass led to Wednesday's second goal against Rotherham in May 1979.

Never-say-die Phil Henson goes where angels fear to tread for Wednesday against Oxford in April 1975. The Owls finished bottom of the Second Division that season.

Sheffield's Sir Andrew Stephen was a giant in football administration in the 70s. Chairman of the Football Association from 1967 to 1976, he was knighted in 1972 for services to football. Dr Stephen became Wednesday's medical officer in 1946 and was chairman of the club from 1956 to 1973. He is pictured at Hillsborough in 1972.

Wednesday held an open day in October 1976 and admiring fans are pictured in the trophy room.

Sixteen-year-old Lorraine Downing, of Chapeltown, Sheffield, a pupil at Notre Dame High School, was chosen as Wednesday's personality girl in 1976 by the Owls Supporters' Club.

The great man himself graced the Hillsborough turf in 1972 when Santos came to play Sheffield Wednesday and this is definitely one for the album as Pele meets Owls personalities including Derek Dooley, Tommy Craig and secretary and general manager Eric Taylor. On the far left of the picture is Tony Pritchett, *The Star's* revered football writer, who died in 2001.

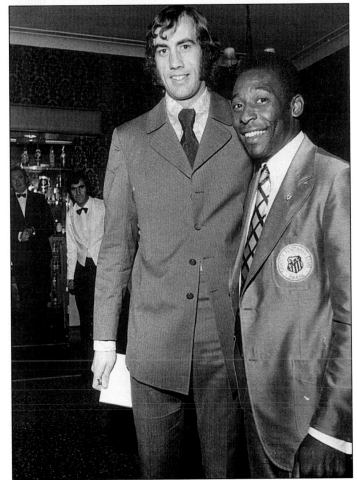

Wednesday hosted the Santos players at the Omega Restaurant, Sheffield, and Pele is pictured with Owls captain John Holsgrove.

A smiling Pele signs autographs for fans at Sheffield's Hallam Tower Hotel.

Pele in action for Santos at Hillsborough.

Wednesday manager Jack Charlton took some of the Wednesday lads up to North Yorkshire to meet his mum, Cissie, in January 1978, and taste some home cooking. Looks like apple pie's on the menu!

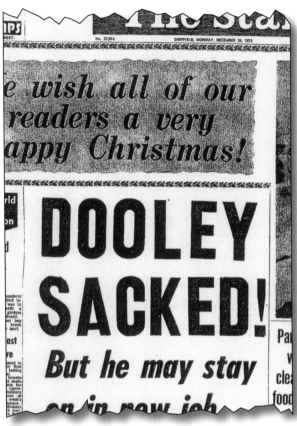

Page One news in *The Star* of Christmas Eve 1973, when Dooley was sacked. He moved across the city and became Sheffield United's commercial manager in 1974, eventually rising to managing director in 1986. After his dismissal from Wednesday, he didn't go near Hillsborough for many years and when he did return it was with United.

Former Wednesday legend Derek Dooley, whose right leg was amputated after an injury against Preston in 1953, was Wednesday's team manager for nearly three years until Christmas Eve 1973 when he lost his job.

Two Sheffield managers in the 70s – United's Ken Furphy on the left with Wednesday's Steve Burtenshaw.

Len Ashurst (right) took over as manager of Third Division Wednesday in October 1975, from Steve Burtenshaw. Ashurst, a no-nonsense Sunderland defender in his playing days, brought with him Tony Toms (left), a former Marine and fitness expert, and the two of them introduced new training procedures. One of the more rigorous disciplines for the players was to spend a night on the moors in January as part of a survival exercise and the experience inspired Ralph Whitworth, *The Star's* brilliant artist, to come up with this classic cartoon.

"I've been roughing it on these moors for years and I'm STILL no good at football!"

Jimmy Sirrell (centre) joined United from Notts County, to where he returned in 1977 after an unsuccessful spell at Bramall Lane. He is pictured here with John Hassall (left) and Bert Jackson.

Jack Charlton, pictured with wife Pat, revived Wednesday's fortunes after joining them in 1977 and within three years they were back in Division Two.

Former miner Danny Williams was Wednesday's manager at the start of the 70s but his reign lasted for less than two years.

The crowd topped 49,000, a Third Division record, for the 1979 Owls v Blades derby. Wednesday won 4-0 and this was their second, a diving header from Terry Curran.

Part of the massive 49,000 – plus crowd at Hillsborough for the 1979 Owls v Blades derby game.

Tommy Craig, at the time Britain's youngest six-figure player (the Owls signed him from Aberdeen for £100,000) leaps in triumph after scoring for Wednesday against United in 1970 but it was United's day. They ran out 3-2 winners, with John Tudor scoring the decider.

Action during the Owls v Blades derby at Hillsborough in 1971. It finished 0-0 and United's point was one of the 56 which took them up to the First Division at the end of that season. Wednesday finished the season in 15th position with 36 points.

Police Horse Loses Eye In Soccer Violence

The 70s football scene in South Yorkshire was scarred by soccer violence, with the area hitting the headlines for all the wrong reasons. The fact that it was part of a national epidemic didn't make it any easier to stomach.

One of the saddest stories concerned police horse Brigadier, who lost an eye during an incident at Barnsley's Oakwell ground.

Letters, get-well cards and presents including boxes of carrots, poured in from all over the country and even abroad. Many were from schoolchildren.

One of the worst outbreaks of violence came in 1974 during Wednesday's Second Division game against Manchester United. More than 60 were injured and 100 arrested, with fighting particularly nasty after the Owls had taken a 3-1 lead. The match finished at 4-4 and that was the season Manchester United got back into the First Division and Wednesday were relegated to the Third.

During an FA Cup semi-final at Hillsborough between Manchester United and Leeds in 1977, nearly 100 fans were arrested and two stabbed.

Staff clean up at the Claymore Hotel, Arundel Gate, Sheffield, after Sheffield United's home match against Newcastle United in 1973. Glasses were smashed, the toilets wrecked and a Christmas stocking collection for the blind stolen.

Mounted police try to sort out crowd trouble at Hillsborough in December 1974 during Wednesday's match against Manchester United. An injured fan is given a piggy-back to safety.

Injured police horse Brigadier pictured with his rider, policeman Neil Blades, at the police stables in Sheffield. Get-well cards adorn the walls and PC Blades holds a box of carrots from a well-wisher.

Police at Hillsborough try to bring down Manchester United fans who had climbed trees before the start of the FA Cup semi-final against Leeds United in 1977. More than 100 fans were arrested during the game.

Cricket Bowled Out At Bramall Lane

Championship cricket at Sheffield United's Bramall Lane football ground was finally bowled out on 7 August 1973. It had been played there since 1855 and the sacred turf, which was sold off to enthusiasts, had been the scene of some legendary landmarks.

It saw some fine centuries over the years, including two in the same match by Geoffrey Boycott against Notts in 1966.

The 70s was a decade of mixed fortunes for the great Yorkshire batsman. He was appointed captain in 1971 and deposed in 1978. In August 1977 he scored his 100th century in first-class cricket, fittingly at Headingley for England against Australia, and in 1978 captained England for three tests in New Zealand.

It's all over at Bramall Lane as cricket enthusiasts leave with chunks of turf.

A cricket ground no more – Bramall Lane becomes a four-sided football ground as Sheffield United's new stand takes shape in May 1975.

Passions ran high in 1978 when Boycott lost the captaincy of Yorkshire and this Yorkshire fan, George Brumpton, of Millhouses, Sheffield, decided to shout his message of support for Boycott from the rooftops. Well, almost – this sign was written on the end of his house.

Geoff Boycott blowing somebody else's trumpet during a benefit night party in 1974. Dave Brennan (second from left) and his well known New Orleans Band provided the jazz as well as a trumpet for Geoff.

On Top Of The World Three Times In 41 Days!

Looking back to 1979, it somehow seems unbelievable that Sheffield athlete Seb Coe broke three world records in 41 days and became the first man to hold, simultaneously, the best times for the 800 and 1500 metres and the mile.

Coe's prowess on the track was becoming apparent as early as 1973 when the 16-year-old lifted the English Schools' 3,000 metres title. By 1977, the former Tapton School pupil was beating established world athletes such as Tanzania's Filbert Bayi to win the Emsley Carr Mile and in 1979 he set up a new world record for the mile of 3 mins 48.9 secs.

A 1976 picture of Coe training in a local park. The date is December 28 and there's a slight covering of snow.

When the city of Sheffield staged a civic dinner for Coe in 1979 and invited along a galaxy of sports stars to celebrate his success, the Lord Mayor of Sheffield, Councillor George Armitage, and the Lady Mayoress, presented him with a set of Sheffield-made carvers. Admiring the gift are Coe's father Peter (second from left) and mother Angela (far right).

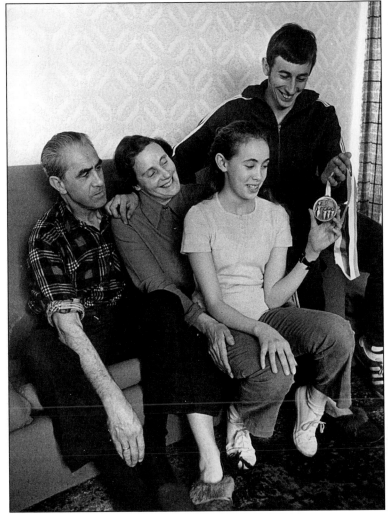

1972 and marathon runner Trevor Wright proudly shows off one of his medals to sister Julie, mum Ida and dad Edwin, at their home in Arbourthorne, Sheffield. Trevor won the silver in the 1971 European Championships.

Angela Creamer competed in the 800 metres at the 1976 Montreal Olympics, represented Great Britain and was national women's 800 metres champion in 1975.

Sheffield walker John Warhurst reads the congratulatory telegrams which poured in after he won a gold medal in the 20-miles event at the 1974 Commonwealth Games.

Sheffield international distance runner and schoolmaster Keith Angus competed in the marathon at the 1976 Montreal Olympics.

Fran Marshall was the world's number one squash player in the 70s, as well as British champion. She also lifted the Yorkshire championship 18 times.

Former Sheffield Parks tennis player Roger Taylor reached the Wimbledon semi-finals three times in the 60s and 70s. One of his most famous victories came in the fourth round at Wimbledon in 1970 when he knocked out the seemingly invincible Rod Laver who hadn't been beaten there since the 1960 final.

Sheffield tennis player Sue Mappin played in nearly all the Wightman Cup matches between 1974-78 and was a Wimbledon doubles semi-finalist twice. She also won the New Zealand Open singles and doubles titles.

Sheffield Hallamshire Golf Club's Mary Everard was British strokeplay champion in 1977 and also captained the Curtis Cup team.

Teachers John and Sheila Sherwood from Sheffield, pictured with daughter Nicola, were awarded MBEs in 1975 for services to athletics. The Queen told them: 'It is not very often that I present awards to a husband and wife at the same time.' Hurdler John and long jumper Sheila both won gold medals in the 1970 Commonwealth Games. Sheila had returned home from the 1968 Mexico Olympics with a silver and John with a bronze, the best ever Olympic husband and wife achievement.

The 1974 Commonwealth Games were a personal triumph for swimmer David Leigh. He won a gold in the 100 metres breaststroke event and a silver in the 200 metres breaststroke. He returned home a hero and colleagues at Sheffield City Swimming Club were among the first to congratulate him.

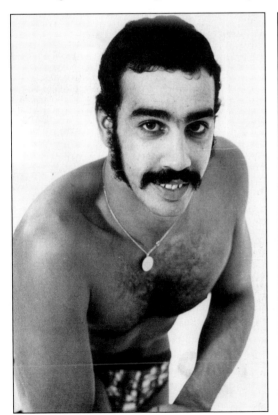

Sheffield City Club freestyle sprint swimmer Kevin Burns, winner of many national events, competed in the 1976 Montreal Olympics.

Now who's this fresh-faced young man just starting out on the path to fame in 1978? None other than Bomber Graham, discovered, like so many good boxers, by Brendan Ingle. Bomber never won a world title but did go on to become British, Commonwealth and European light middleweight champion and also European middleweight champion.

Subscribers

1. Mr David Edmondson
2. Michelle Jackson
3. James Larkin
4. Mr David James Gains
5. Margaret Maxfield
6. Gary Grimes
7. Ian Douglas Tevendale
8. Raymond Keith Longden
9. Mrs Annie Maria Weston
10. Mr Peter E. Bradshaw
11. Alan Thornton
12. Richard Hobson
13. Levick Family
14. Mary Haigh Glover
15. Paul Watson
16. L.M. Degenhart
17. Kathryn Dumelow
18. Roy Young
19. David Ibberson
20. John Broughton
21. Susan Roberts
22. Edgar Eastwood
23. Jennifer Mary McDermott
24. Anthony W. Rider
25. Graham & Carolyn Spurr
26. Simon & Deborah Spurr
27. Mark, Amanda & Laura Graves
28. Patricia A. Bowles
29. Margaret Walker
30. Edwin Speight
31. Jessie G. Grayson
32. Mr & Mrs A.R. Carr
33. Emma Stephenson
34. Tracey Anderson
35. Ian Douglas Tevendale
36. Mrs B.A. Hossell
37. Gordon Frederick Wakefield
38. Craig Colton
39. Eric Shipley
40. Nigel Richard Deane
41. Ruth Barber
42. John Michael Naylor
43. Sheila Clark
44. Neil Andrew Stringer
45. June Hardcastle
46. Robert Michael Prestwood
47. Gary Bartram
48. Andrew Speight
49. Paul & Sara Speight
50. Richard & Carol Speight
51. Harvey Reynolds
52. Mick Melia
53. Roy White
54. Terry Jackson
55. Keith M. Cotterill
56. Stephen Adcock
57. Robert Firth
58. Mavis Lem
59. Roger Fidment
60. Kathleen & Farrel Smith
61. Glyn Wood
62. David Wood
63. Audrey E. Bark
64. Harry Shillito
65. Joshua Cooper
66. Lesley Waller
67. Mrs Beryl Ann Johnson
68. Gordon Hodgkinson
69. Peter Simpson
70. Annie Vilma Jeffries
71. Roger Michael Battye
72. Anita Cole
73. Robert Whitham
74. Kathleen Elaine Rhodes
75. Mr William (Wills) Smith
76. Frank David Gee
77. Jack Barnett
78. John Mitchell
79. Anthony James Cawthorne
80. Cyril King
81. Raymond Allwood
82. Mark Hatfield
83. J. Barry Swift
84. Mr Brian Gregory
85. Mr Robert W. Spencer
86. Derek Tingle
87. Janet Toulson
88. Lorraine Hardy
89. Sue Eastwood
90. Margaret Bannister
91. Gordon W. Bell
92. Michael J. Crossland
93. David Leslie Heighington
94. Michael Peter Brookes
95. Desmond Pass
96. Elaine R. Rennie
97. Jim Pratt
98. Howard John Goodison
99. Mrs Joan Naylor
100. Nicola Anderson
101. Daniel Cole
102. Matthew Cole
103. Alan Hainsworth
104. Annette Gillott
105. Morcia Kay Platt
106. John B. Sutcliffe
107. Helen Bingham (née Austick)
108. Katrina Milley (née Bingham)
109. Patrick T. Widdowson
110. Philip Andrew Stanley
111. Mr Paul Casbolt
112. Simon Hinchcliffe
113. Steve Goulding
114. Mr John William Stocks
115. B. D. Allen
116. D. K. Hardy
117. A. J. Hardy
118. Mr Barry Kay
119. Brian Thompson
120. Brian Darwent
121. Anthony Stephen Wallis
122. Harry Parker
123. Edward Cavanagh
124. Peter D. Brand
125. Gordon Gregory
126. Linda Christine Bell
127. Peter Roche
128. Simon Stead
129. Alice Pierce
130. Phil Cotterill
131. Graham Marshall
132. John Mark Oakley
133. Graham Briggs
134. Mr Michael Byrne
135. Jenny Hannah
136. Carol Sorby
137. J. McKendrick
138. Derek Ellis
139. Steven Kennedy
140. Greg Chapman
141. Christine Priest
142. Gerald G. Hall
143. Matloub Husayn-Ali-Khan
144. Steve Cryan
145. Linda Mitchell